better together*

*This book is best read together, grownup and kid.

 akidsco.com

a
kids
book
about

a kids book about Heritage Languages

by Anita K. Sachariah

a kids book about

Text and design copyright © 2024
by A Kids Book About, Inc.

Copyright is good! It ensures that work like this can exist, and more work in the future can be created.

All rights reserved. No part of this publication may be reproduced, distributed, or transmitted in any form or by any means, including photocopying, recording, other electronic or mechanical methods, without the prior written permission of the publisher, except in the case of brief quotations embodied in critical reviews and certain other noncommercial uses permitted by copyright law. For permission requests, write to the publisher.

A Kids Book About, Kids Are Ready, and the colophon 'a' are trademarks of A Kids Book About, Inc.

Printed in the United States of America.

A Kids Book About books are available online: *akidsco.com*

To share your stories, ask questions, or inquire about bulk purchases (schools, libraries, and nonprofits), please use the following email address: *hello@akidsco.com*

Print ISBN: 979-8-89281-059-3
Ebook ISBN: 979-8-89281-060-9

Designed by Rick DeLucco
Edited by Emma Wolf

For anyone who lost their language:
may you find it again.

For my husband, Arun, and kids, Arjun and Ananya:
you inspire me to try hard things.

In memory of my loving parents, who tried their best.

Intro

Language is not just about specific words and communication. Languages connect us to our heritage and culture.

When a family moves to a country where their native language is not spoken, they are likely to lose it. This is especially true in monolingual countries, where it is usual to speak only 1 language, typically English. By the third generation, this family is likely to speak only English at home. Their heritage language becomes a memory.

When we lose the ability to speak our languages, we lose a vital connection to our families, our history, our culture, and homeland. Yet for immigrants, their children, and grandchildren, heritage language is central to our identity.

This book is meant to help kids feel pride in having a heritage language. It encourages them to learn their languages while acknowledging some of the challenges they may face along the way. I hope my story inspires kids and grownups to begin their language journey.

What language do you hear spoken around you every day?

What language do you use?

Is it different at school than it is at home?

Is it different between your grandparents, your parents, or you?

You may hear mostly
1 language spoken.

Hindi, Mandarin Chinese, Malayalam, Spanish, French, Arabic, Navajo, Bengali, Amharic, Portuguese, Russian, Urdu, Tagalog, Indonesian, German, Japanese, Yoruba, Marathi, Telugu, Turkish, Tamil, Vietnamese, Korean,

You may hear different languages spoken.

Italian, Persian, Hausa, Swahili, Javanese, Hebrew, Punjabi, Haitian Creole, Gujarati, Thai, Kannada, Cherokee, Hawaiian, Dutch, English, Romanian, Swahili, Yiddish, Swedish, American sign language...

And maybe, you're surrounded by people who know

many differe

nt languages.

Have you heard the term **"bilingual"**?

That means someone speaks
2 languages really well.

But there are different
types of bilingual people.

Some people study to learn a second language, and learn it from the very beginning.

Other people are born into a family who already speak another language.

This is called a...

language.

A language you inherit from your family.

You may still need to study
your heritage language to learn it.

In some ways, doing so can be easier compared to someone who learns from scratch.

But in some ways, it can be harder.

Let me explain why!

If you have a heritage language, have you ever felt embarrassed or ashamed to speak it?

Maybe because you don't want to make mistakes in front of your family.

Maybe because no one else outside of your family speaks the same language.

Maybe you're afraid of getting made fun of for speaking a language which is different from everyone else's.

People with a heritage language can sometimes feel disconnected from both their culture and the society they live in—like they exist somewhere between them.

I often felt this way because I didn't learn my own heritage language, **Malayalam**,* well enough to speak it.

*Malayalam is a language spoken by over 40 million people. It is primarily spoken in the southern part of India, in the state of Kerala, but also by Malayali people around the world.

My parents, Aunties, and religious community all spoke it…and I often felt left out.

I knew a little bit, but not enough to communicate as quickly as I do in English. I was embarrassed to speak Malayalam in front of my family.

Have you ever felt like this?

You are not alone!

I was also embarrassed to speak Malayalam around my classmates or outside of my house.

I didn't want to sound different from my friends.

Instead of calling my mother "Amma" (a word for "Mom" in Malayalam), I would call her "Mommy."

When you change the words you use and how you speak to fit in and so others will understand you better, it's called code switching.

It can definitely seem
more convenient at times.

But you don't have to hide who
you are from your family or society.

You can live fully in both your inherited culture and the culture you are growing up in without having to choose.

You are

both.

If you want to learn
your heritage language,

that's awesome!

Learning your heritage language will not hurt your English.

In fact, kids have super brains that make learning languages easier.

So this is a **great** time to start!

And who said learning has to be boring?

It's so much better when it's fun!

You can:

play games,

read bilingual books,

take a class,

use flashcards,

have a playdate with other kids who speak your language, or

watch cartoons in your language!

You can:

- learn nursery ryhmes

- try new recipes

- sing songs

- build crafts

- listen to podcasts

- put together puzzles

- dance to music

- read books

Maybe you can even travel to the country where your family is from!

There are SO many ways to connect with your heritage language.

There is no perfect way to learn, and it takes many years to become fluent.*

*Fluent means you can speak, understand, read, and write a language easily and without mistakes.

When you hear your heritage language, do you understand it?

Do you want to speak it? Are you curious about how to read and write in your language?

That's up to you! Each of these skills take different amounts of time and effort to learn.

So, start as soon as you can, and be patient!

Learning a heritage language also takes courage.

Other people may not treat your language with the respect it deserves.

Be brave. Don't believe them.

There are thousands of languages spoken around the world, and each one matters.

Your language is beautiful, has a long history, connects you to your family, and connects you to another part of this big world.

What happens if we don't learn these languages?

Sadly, they may *disappear*

But you have the power to keep your heritage language...

You won't regret learning your language (I promise).

But you may regret not learning it (that's what happened to me!).

Now, as a grownup, I'm studying Malayalam and it fills my heart.

And the best part is, I remember things from when I was a kid that help me learn faster now!

Growing up, I often felt sad, like something was missing.

But now, by honoring my desire to learn and connect with my heritage language, I've found that lost piece.

So, what's your heritage language?

And how will

you honor it?

Outro

Nanni നന്ദി. Nandri நன்றி. Dhanyavaad धन्यवाद. Gracias. Merci. Thank you for reading this book!

Heritage languages are not just academic. They are psychological, rooted in emotion and longing. Acknowledging this is key to progress.

Now that you know what a heritage language is and what makes it special, what will you do next? I hope you feel empowered to start your heritage language journey. And on this journey, practice patience, try many different ways to learn, and be brave.

Grownups, now is your chance to share your language story, including both the roses and thorns you experienced along the way. What was it like for you?

Maybe you aren't a fluent speaker, but know enough to get by at family events. You don't have to be fluent for your kids to learn. In fact, you can learn with your kids. Make languages a part of your everyday life. Language is a gift your kid will carry with them all their life.

About The Author

Anita K. Sachariah (she/her) is the founder of BhashaKids, which exists to connect the South Asian diaspora with their heritage languages. A mom and educator, Anita started BK after feeling frustrated by the lack of quality language products to help her own kids. So, she set out to create them herself.

Her work includes creating and curating bilingual and inclusive language learning materials for kids, coaching parents, language teachers, and schools, as well as promoting bilingual books and South Asian kidlit.

Raised in the USA by South Indian parents, Anita speaks English, French, and some Spanish. She is now (re)learning Malayalam, her heritage language, as well as Tamil, her husband's language. You can hear Tamil, Malayalam, Hindi, and Spanish (along with English) spoken in her multicultural home.

 @bhashakids   @bhashakids   bhashakids.com

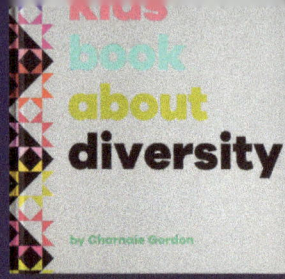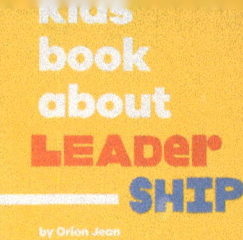
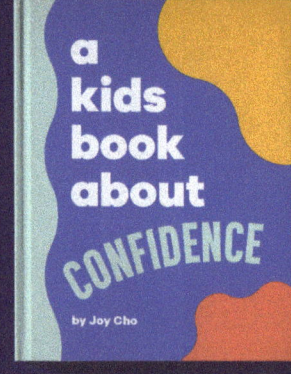

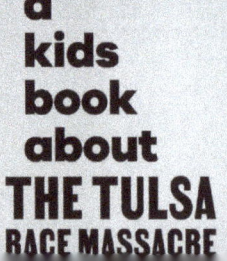

Discover more at akidsco.com